M is for Mary

Dr. C. White-Elliott

Illustrated by Nicholas Harrison

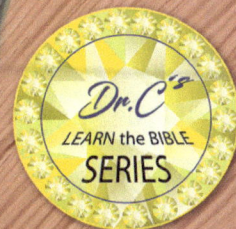

www.clfpublishing.org
909.315.3161

Cover design by Senir Design. Contact info: info@senirdesign.com

Illustrated by Nicholas Harrison.

ISBN #978-1-945102-63-9

Printed in the United States of America.

For

Kori Parker

"For unto us a child is born, unto us a son is given: and the government shall be upon his shoulder: and his name shall be called Wonderful, Counseller, The mighty God, The everlasting Father, Prince of Peace."

Isaiah 9:6

"Therefore the Lord Himself will give you a sign:

Behold, the virgin shall conceive and bear a Son,

and shall call His name Immanuel."

Isaiah 7:14

In a village called Nazareth, the angel Gabriel went to visit a teenage girl named Mary. When the angel appeared before Mary, he said, "Greetings. You are favored of God. The Lord is with you."

Mary was very confused. She did not know why the angel would visit her, and she did not know what his words meant. Gabriel could tell Mary was confused, so he said, "Don't be afraid, Mary. You have found favor with God." Mary did not answer. She stayed quiet as the angel spoke.

Gabriel told Mary, "You will give birth to a son, and you will name him Jesus. He will be called the Son of the Most High. He will reign over Israel, from the throne of David. His kingdom will never end."

Mary still did not understand all the angel was telling her. She asked, "How can I have a baby when I am a virgin?"

Gabriel said, "The Holy Spirit will come upon you, and the power of God will overshadow you."

Mary answered, "I am the Lord's servant. Let everything you said about me come true."

Then, the angel left.

When the time came for Mary to give birth to her son, she and her fiancé Joseph were in Bethlehem. There were no hospitals at that time, and no inns were available. So, Mary gave birth to her son in a stable. She wrapped him in a cloth and placed him in a manger. She named her son Jesus.

The shepherds made their way to find the newborn baby boy. When they left him, they went and told everyone the good news. Later, wise men visited King Jesus, leaving many gifts: gold, frankincense, and myrrh.

Mary loved her baby boy, and she was honored that God had chosen her to be the mother of the Savior of the world. From that day forward, many people would call upon the name of Jesus, and through Him, they would be saved from their sins.

www.ingramcontent.com/pod-product-compliance
Lightning Source LLC
Chambersburg PA
CBHW041957100426
42813CB00019B/2911